PRECIOUS MEMORIES

BY MARVIN LEE PARMER

Look for the good things,
embrace the memories,
and have at least
one moment of hope.

Title: Precious Memories

Author: Marvin Lee Parmer

© Marvin Lee Parmer February 23, 2013

Publisher: Dr. Jim A. Talley
R&R Publishing, Inc.
11805 Sylvester Dr.
Oklahoma City, OK 73162-1018
(405) 822-8300
Web: www.drtalley.com
Email: drtalley@drtalley.com
Twitter: drtalley42

Editor: Paula Corley
Jot and Tittle Editing
9005 North Mac Arthur Terrace
Oklahoma City, OK 73132-2816
(405) 721-7741
Email: pacorley@sbcglobal.net

Designer: Phillip Grimes
The Creative Guy, Inc.
(405) 496-6151
Email: okcdesigner@gmail.com

Illustrator: Joyce Talley
Original Art, Inc.
11805 Sylvester Dr.
Oklahoma City, OK 73162-1018
(405) 822-8300
Web: www.drtalley.com
Email: drtalley@drtalley.com
Twitter: drtalley42

PRECIOUS MEMORIES

Precious memories, unseen angels,
Sent from somewhere to my soul;
How they linger, ever near me,
And the sacred past unfold.

Precious memories how they linger,
How they ever flood my soul;
In the stillness of the midnight,
Precious, sacred scenes unfold.

Precious father, loving mother,
Lie across the lonely years, and
From the home scene of my childhood,
Precious memories flood my soul.

Precious memories how they linger,
How they ever flood my soul;
In the stillness of the midnight,
Precious, sacred scenes unfold.

As I travel on life's pathway,
I know not what the years may hold;
As I ponder, hope grows fonder,
Precious memories flood my soul.

Precious memories how they linger,
How they ever flood my soul;
In the stillness of the midnight,
Precious, sacred scenes unfold.

Things I Have Learned

Love, not time, heals all wounds.

Everyone you meet
deserves to be greeted with a smile.

The Lord didn't do it all in one day.

Under everyone's hard shell
is a person who wants to be
appreciated and loved.

Life is tough, but with God's help,
I can handle it.

DEDICATED TO

*My loving wife, who has loved me
and stood by me since 12-18-1948*

*Mom and Pop Parmer, who taught me
about life and the Lord Jesus Christ*

IN THE BEGINNING

It was a winter-type day with drifting clouds in the sky. Leaves on the trees were changing color and falling to the ground. For those who loved this time of year, it was a beautiful day. It was Sunday November 13, 1927, the beginning of my life.

My mother was Threcy Rose Lee Carter Parmer. Her parents were Wylie and Sally Carter. They had five boys: Roe, Ulis, Lewis, Clarence, and Robert. I was told, my mother being the only girl in the family, that she was very spoiled. Could it be that a young lady with five brothers could be spoiled?

The Carter home was located near Greenwood, Arkansas, in a community called Lone Star. Communities existed throughout the rural areas. Each consisted of a public building near the center of the area that was used for a church and a school. Nearby towns provided a place to buy what was needed and to sell produce.

My dad, Marvin Tensely Parmer, son of John Lewis Parmer and Dora Ann Rush Parmer, was one of seven boys: Norman, Virgil, Marvin, Thurman, Otto, Otho, and Loren. My dad grew up in the community of Sulphur Springs, which was also near Greenwood, Arkansas. The two communities were four to five miles apart.

I do not know how my parents met each other or what kind of contact they had during their courting years. In those days transportation was limited to riding on a horse or in a horse-drawn buggy. Communication by telephone was confined to certain areas. Community telephones were party lines; this allowed anyone who so desired to listen to your conversation. It was really romantic, don't you think?

After my parents were married, they moved to Paris, Arkansas, where Dad worked in a coal mine. As the time for my birth drew near, Mother and Dad went to her parents' home for my delivery. Each town had a doctor who made house calls for emergencies, such as delivering babies. Dr. Hall, whose office was in Greenwood, was called to attend my birth.

I was born on a kitchen table in my maternal grandparents' home. Kitchen tables in those days were usually long rectangles, suitable for seating the entire family. The whole family ate meals together, at the same time, and teaching and learning were part of each meal. Everyone learned the sequential arrangement of God, family, and work.

The Lord God, Father of heaven and earth, gave me life. But He took my mother to heaven to dwell with Him forever. After this, my dad took me to live with his mother and dad. From that time on, my paternal grandparents became Mom and Pop to me.

Mom and Pop owned and lived on a farm seven miles east of Greenwood, Arkansas, in the Fairview community in Sebastian County. Like other communities Fairview was privileged to have a centrally located building where we met for church. Our church was of the Baptist belief. We met Sunday morning for Sunday school and a preaching service. In the evening we met for Baptist Young People's Union, or BYPU, to learn how to apply the Bible to different life situations. BYPU was followed by another preaching service.

We lived one mile from the church, so we usually walked to get there. The road was a dirt road that passed our house and proceeded straight to the church and beyond. Occasionally it got dark before we left church to walk home. Then our light to see the road came only from the moon and stars. It was our life, and we were thankful for what we had.

Our church pastor lived in a neighboring community about four or five miles away. He lived with his wife in a rental house on a small acreage. He was not called to be a farmer, but he was called by God to be a preacher of God's holy Word. He commuted, via an old automobile, from his house to the church house every Sunday morning. After the Sunday morning service, he frequently came to our house for lunch and to stay until the evening church service.

Cash money was very limited in those days. Church members were only able to save a few pennies for a cash offering but supplemented the cash with produce from their farms. This was during the Great Depression, and earning a living was very hard.

We observed the birth of Jesus Christ on Christmas Day, but I don't remember details about celebrating Christmas with a lot of gifts. I do remember my dad gave me a little red wagon when I was seven or eight years old. I really did enjoy playing with it.

There was a ridge of hills that lay just across the road from our house. I often pulled the little red wagon up the hill and rode it down the hill for a distance of about thirty or forty yards. It was fun except when the wagon turned over and I landed on a cactus! The plant was a prickly pear cactus, which had very fine needles that enjoyed penetrating your clothing and your skin. To remove the needles, someone rubbed a small piece of sandstone over the contaminated area of your clothing and your body. It was effective in removing the needles, but it did irritate the skin.

In the rural area where we lived, there was some distance

between houses, one quarter to one-half mile, and social life was limited. On designated Sundays people brought food to church, and a picnic was in order after the morning service. I enjoyed these occasions because they were opportunities to taste foods that were different from those we ate at home. Remember, restaurants and hamburger drive-ins were not available to us. On other occasions people might plan socials at their homes. The hosts organized games that allowed interaction between boys and girls to help them get acquainted.

Every now and then someone held an ice cream social. People brought their hand-cranked ice cream freezers with their ice cream mix, ready to freeze. Ice was purchased in town and transported to the party, frozen in large blocks consisting of a conglomerate of smaller 25-pound blocks. Thus the ice could be purchased in increments of 25, 50, 75, and 100 pounds.

Keeping the ice from melting before it could be used was a big problem. We wrapped the blocks in bed quilts and tarpaulin sheets to help reduce melting. Then we used an ice pick to chip the ice into small pieces so the freezer could be filled with ice.

An ice cream freezer consisted of a metal canister and lid that fit inside a cylindrical wooden bucket. Chips of ice filled the void between canister and bucket. A hand-cranked mechanism rotated the metal canister containing the ice cream mix. The cranking action always caused the freezer to move around on the ground, so my contribution was to hold the freezer steady by sitting on it.

We didn't have any way to keep leftover ice, so we used all of it. We sure could have used an icebox, which was the forerunner to today's refrigerator. A large number of city residents owned iceboxes, so the ice plant was located in town. Ice could, therefore, be delivered to the residents with a minimum amount of melting.

The first icebox I saw belonged to my Uncle Thurman and Aunt Irene Parmer, who lived in Fort Smith, Arkansas. A horse-drawn wagon delivered ice to their home. Bottled milk was also delivered by a horse-drawn milk wagon. Boy, did I think that was great!

Without ice, there was no ice water or iced tea to drink. The few times I was privileged to visit my Uncle Norman and Aunt Bertha Parmer in east Texas, one of the highlights of our visit was the iced tea my aunt served. Small, simple things meant so much to me.

By the time I was of school age, the school district had consolidated the community schools into the Greenwood School District. A school bus picked me up in front of my house to transport me the seven miles to and from school. I point this out because in my world at that time, very few people owned a car. Most transportation was still by horse and buggy, and my grandparents did not own a car.

Just how far is seven miles? It is 36,960 feet, and if you cover two and one-half feet per step, that is 14,784 steps. I learned this the hard way when I missed the school bus one afternoon. I might add that I never missed the school bus again. One never forgets a lesson learned the hard way. Isn't education wonderful? It comes in different ways.

Thanks to transportation today, the time it takes to cover seven miles is very short. If you want to go across town, the distance is of little concern; you get into the car, start the engine, put it in gear, and are on your way. Ten to twelve minutes later, you have covered seven miles. Compare this to traveling by horse. The horse must be caught, bridled, and saddled. It may object to this treatment, so travel time varies depending on the time required to overcome the horse's objections. To travel seven miles may take forty minutes or more.

The moral to this story is: If you are in a hurry, own a good running automobile.

LIFE ON THE FARM

In our area of the country, electricity, gas, and running water were not available. Kerosene-burning lamps and lanterns provided our light, and heat came from burning wood in a fireplace or a cast-iron stove. Air conditioning had never been heard of.

Life on the farm consisted of rising early, usually at five o'clock in the morning. While Mom prepared breakfast and my lunch for school, I helped Pop and my uncles feed the livestock and milk the cows. Afterward we let the cows out to pasture where they could graze. In the evening we herded them back to the barn for feeding and another milking.

When a milking was finished, we carried the milk in buckets to the milk house to be processed through a hand-cranked separator, which extracted the cream from the milk. We made butter from the cream and sold the milk, giving us another source of income. Each day a truck came to our house and picked up the milk cans we had filled and transported them to a dairy processing facility in Greenwood to be made into cheese. The cans were returned the next day for us to refill.

As my contribution to the milk business, I had the job of cranking the separator. There were occasions when there was some disagreement between us boys. One time Uncle Loren and I were involved in a little skirmish, and he accidentally hit me on my right elbow with a hoe. The result was pain when I bent my elbow. Hoping to keep himself out of trouble, Uncle Loren offered to crank the separator if I wouldn't tell Mom. Boy, I had it made for a while!

Each spring we prepared the fields and planted. In the summer we cultivated the plants that had come up, and in the fall we enjoyed the harvest. We grew the food needed to sustain us: apples, peaches, and grapes and a vegetable garden of foods such as tomatoes, turnips, okra, beans, radishes, lettuce, cabbage, cucumbers, peas, corn, carrots, and onions. We had fresh vegetables to eat all summer!

In preparation for the winter months, we canned vegetables and fruit. Believe me, the canning process was labor intensive! We cleaned and sterilized the reusable glass jars with boiling water heated in a metal tub over an open wood-burning fire. The food itself was cooked on a wood-burning cast-iron stove located in the kitchen. Since it was summer, the weather was hot, and the canning process generated even more heat. Air conditioning would have been a blessing had it been available.

One of my favorite food-related memories is of the jellies and preserves we canned using our peaches, strawberries, and grapes. Just remembering how very tasty these jams were with fresh-baked biscuits and butter causes me to salivate even now!

Once the canning was finished, we needed to protect all those jars from the summer heat. Taking advantage of the fact that the temperature of the soil remained cooler below a certain depth, we constructed a dirt cellar. First we dug a hole in the ground. Next we built a roof over the hole and spread soil over it to form a spherical shape to cause rainwater to drain away. A door in the side of the hole allowed us to enter and exit. Finally, we stacked our bounty of jars on shelves built against the walls inside the cellar.

The cellar could also be used as a storm cellar when conditions warranted. But there was a downside: Spiders inhabited the cellar, and they really didn't like to share it with us. I don't remember anyone becoming ill from spider bites, but it may have happened.

Pork and chicken were our primary meat courses, and we raised both hogs and chickens. Chickens provided eggs, both for our consumption and to sell at the market. The money we earned from selling eggs helped us buy staples such as sugar and flour. Flour usually came in white cloth sacks, which were used to make underclothes for both men and women. Some flour sacks were made of colored prints and florals, which were turned into clothing such as women's dresses.

When cool weather arrived, usually in November, it was time to slaughter the hogs. Neighbor helped neighbor with the process of cleaning the carcass and cutting it into parts: pork chops, ham, ribs, bacon, backbone, shoulder, and sausage. Excess fat was trimmed from these parts and cooked in a large cast-iron pot to obtain lard or shortening to be used in seasoning other foods or making laundry soap. Once the fat was rendered, what was left was called *cracklings*, a crunchy substance shaped like popcorn that could be used in cornbread mix to add flavor (thus the term *crackling corn bread*).

Because we had no means of refrigeration, we packed the pork in salt to preserve it. Each farm had a smokehouse, a small building similar to a one-car garage and set apart from any other building. The smokehouse was an enclosed structure with a door, exposed rafters, and a dirt floor. Large wooden salt boxes with top-mounted lids lined the inside walls of the smokehouse. Meat was layered in the boxes, with salt packed all around it. This kept the meat cool and prevented spoiling. Other meat was suspended from the rafters while hickory wood smoldered in a firebox sitting on the floor. The smoke both cured and added flavor to the meat.

Beef was not suited for this type of preservation. Therefore, we sold selected beef stock to make money to buy other things we needed.

INCOME

Our primary source of income was cotton. We planted cotton seed in the spring with a horse-drawn, single-row planter. When the cotton plants started growing, they had to be thinned out to a few inches apart. We did this manually with a cotton hoe, one row at a time; this was called *chopping cotton.* To keep the weeds from smothering the cotton plants, we plowed between the rows with a horse-drawn plow and followed that with hoeing the weeds from around the cotton plants.

Since our consolidated school was populated by mostly farm people, school did not begin until after the cotton was harvested in September. We hand-picked the cotton and placed it in large canvas sacks that we pulled alongside and behind us by a strap over our shoulders. This kept both hands free to pick the cotton. As the sacks were filled, we dragged or carried them to a scale where the cotton was weighed and dumped into a wagon. When the wagon was full, a horse pulled it to the cotton gin in Greenwood. There the cotton was compressed into large, rectangular-shaped bales to be stacked with other bales on a railroad car and shipped to the mills that produced fabric.

I had no knowledge of mechanical engineering, but I dreamed of the day when someone would invent a machine for picking cotton. Someone did—after I left the farm.

We were paid by the pound for the cotton. This income was enough for us to buy shoes and clothing for the following year. As a result we learned to be very careful in how we treated our clothing.

Corn was another crop we raised. It was planted and cultivated in a similar manner to the cotton, and hoeing and plowing helped control the weeds. In the fall of the year, we harvested the corn. In the process, a horse pulled a wagon along the rows as people walked beside it, pulling the ears of corn from the stalks by hand and tossing them into the wagon.

The corn was stored in a building called a *corn crib*, which could be free-standing or contained in a barn. It was built to allow air to circulate through it, drying the corn to keep it from molding and ultimately rotting. As the corn was needed for making other products, we pulled off the shucks by hand and then fed the ears into a hand-cranked machine that removed the kernels from the cob. The corn could then be taken to a mill to be ground into cornmeal. Or it could be mixed with other ingredients to make food for the livestock.

Sugar cane was another of our crops. We fed the harvested cane stalks through a roller mill that squeezed the liquid from the stalk to be processed into molasses. To produce food for the livestock, we mixed what was left of the stalks with other ingredients.

Not all of our farm was used for growing crops. We also dedicated a plot of land to the purpose of growing grass. In this hay meadow we cut and processed the grass into bales that could be manually lifted onto a horse-drawn wagon and transported to the hay barn. There we unloaded and stacked the bales to protect them from the weather and provide winter food for the livestock.

As mentioned before, we also earned some income from selling eggs. Our chickens lived in a hen house, which consisted of rows of built-in open boxes, mounted above ground. Each box contained some hay for the hens to sit on and lay eggs in. Each day we reached under the hens and collected the eggs they had laid. Then on most Saturdays we hitched a team of horses to the wagon and drove into the town of Greenwood. There we could sell the eggs and purchase other supplies.

Going to town was really a treat! At Ellis's Grocery Store we sold our eggs and purchased needed supplies. Pop always gave me a dime and a nickel to buy my lunch. I purchased some cheese and crackers with the dime and a bottle of root beer with the nickel. Then I went to the back of the store where the feed sacks were stored, sat on one of the sacks, and ate my lunch. Later, if I was fortunate to find my Uncle Dutch Carter, he bought me an ice cream cone. Life was good!

Downtown Greenwood was built in a rectangular shape around a town square. A nice little park near the center of the square was adorned with large trees that offered cool shade from the summer heat. Park benches provided a place to sit, rest, and visit with other people.

State Highway 10 ran east and west through the center of town. It did not divide the park but made a semicircle around the south side of the park. The county courthouse was a free-standing building located south of the semicircle. Storefronts were built along the other three sides, facing the square. People moved in and out of the stores into the park. The area was relatively small, so it was easy to see people you knew—like Uncle Dutch!

Next door to Ellis's Grocery Store was a movie theater. Ellis gave free tickets to his customers' children for the Saturday afternoon matinee. On one of those trips to town I viewed my first movie. It was a silent movie but a great thrill for me because I didn't know movies existed!

RECREATION

A spring-fed creek crossed our farm, flowing from west to east. Water ran in the creek most of the year except during the hot summer time. Even then, there was movement enough to keep the water from becoming stagnant. This creek formed a pool in the middle of our farm, and it served as our "swimming pool." For a treat we carried warm watermelons from the field to our pool and deposited them in the water to cool while we swam. Even though they were not truly cold, we enjoyed eating them.

When the water was clear and flowing in the creek, we also used it for bathing. At other times we bathed in washtubs. When the weather was warm we filled the tubs with fresh well water and set them in the sunshine to warm the water. During cool weather, we heated water on a wood-burning stove. Mom believed that cleanliness was next to godliness.

The soil between the house and the water well was very sandy and an excellent place to pitch horseshoes. For this we used worn horseshoes. None of them weighed the same, nor were they balanced. But they made for an interesting game.

Shooting marbles was a popular game among the boys at school. To play, we drew a circle on the ground, approximately four feet in diameter, and deposited a number of marbles in the center of the circle. Each player chose a marble to use as his shooting marble and took a turn at trying to shoot marbles outside the circle. To launch the shooting marble from his hand, the player held the marble in the crook of his forefinger and used his thumb to shoot the marble forward in a motion similar to snapping one's finger. A player's turn ended when he failed to shoot a marble from the circle. The game continued until all marbles had been removed from the circle. The winner was the one who had collected the most marbles.

Another game we played was football. Uncle Loren once came up with a football cover from somewhere. The bladder was missing, so he filled the cover with cotton seed, which made it very heavy. This meant that whenever I caught a pass, the impact of that football usually knocked me down. But we had fun.

In Greenwood, a town of approximately 1200 people, a new swimming pool—much larger than the one on our farm—was available. This pool was one mile south of town and formed in Bryanie Creek. A large oak tree grew on its bank, and someone had hung a rope from a large branch that extended over the pool. We could pull the rope back to the bank of the creek, grab on to it, swing out over the water, and dive in.

On occasion, some of my school friends and I went swimming in the nude. We were used to doing this in the pool on our farm, and it didn't occur to us that other people, including females, also swam in this pool. We were soon enlightened, however, when a group of people showed up to swim and presented us with an embarrassing situation. From then on we decided it would be a good idea to take off our clothes upstream, where we could hide them in the underbrush and then swim to the pool. If someone showed up, we could escape by swimming up-stream to our clothing.

My family was not blessed with musical talent. Church was the primary place for us to sing, but Mom and I often sang hymns as we worked in the house. Our housework was punctuated by the strains of hymns such as "Amazing Grace," "The Old Rugged Cross," and "Leaning on the Everlasting Arms."

My exposure to music was very limited because we didn't have any musical instruments in the house, and I was twelve or thirteen years old before we were blessed with a battery-powered radio. But one of our neighbors had musical talent and was able to play most of the stringed instruments, a pump organ, and a mouth harp. Despite the neighbor's efforts to teach me, I had no success at learning to play the mouth harp.

In my early teenage years, I liked country-western music. The Grand Ole Opry was a favorite. Over the years, some of the performers I have liked best have been Patsy Cline, Loretta Lynn, Johnny Cash, Willie Nelson, Bing Crosby, Frank Sinatra, and Big Band Era performers like Glenn Miller, Tommy Dorsey, Harry James, and Benny Goodman.

NEIGHBORS

Adjoining our farm on the east side was the farm belonging to Mr. and Mrs. George Hearn. Mr. Hearn grew grapes from which he made wine for his own use. His grandson, Lee, was my age, but he and his family didn't live permanently in our area. At different seasons of the year Lee and his family came to help Mr. and Mrs. Hearn on the farm.

When Mr. Hearn made his wine, he put it in glass fruit jars and stored them in a cellar. One day when I was about twelve years old, Lee sneaked out a pint jar of wine and gave it to me. I sure did not want Mom and Pop to know about it and needed a place to hide it. Since there was a spring of cool, flowing water located on the hill in front of our house, it seemed logical to hide the wine there.

Gerald Parmer, my cousin who was three years older than I, occasionally came to visit. One time I told him about the wine, and he suggested we drink it. So when the opportunity came, we retrieved the wine from the spring and imbibed. We thought we were really cool and were ready to bring on the caviar!

Now if a pint was this good, we thought, a quart would be wonderful. So we asked Lee to bring us a quart when he could sneak one out. By the time he accomplished this, though, summer had arrived and the mercury in the thermostat had risen. When I took the wine to deposit in my hiding place, the spring had dried up. There was no cool water. Looking around for another secret place, I spied a pile of brush nearby. It looked like a good location, and I deposited the jar of wine there.

Of course, by this point I felt very knowledgeable in the art of making and preserving wine. When the right time came, Gerald and I retrieved the jar of wine and proceeded to our private hiding place, a concrete road culvert located one hundred yards east of our barn. There was ample space inside for us to sit and sample our wine. But in all of my acquired knowledge of winemaking, I had missed something: Grapes contained in a fruit jar and exposed to high temperature continue to ferment or rot. So when I drank a large gulp from the quart jar that had been hidden in the brush, I almost immediately lost my previous meal. For the next ten years I had no desire to taste any wine.

Another neighbor, Mrs. Lockridge, was a widow who lived approximately one mile west of our farm. Her husband had fought in the Spanish-American War, and upon his death, she was left with two sons, who were ten or twelve years my senior and did not live with her. One lived in California, and the other was in the United States Navy. This was, probably, the first time I heard there was a Navy.

As I remember, Mrs. Lockridge was the only one in the community with a grass lawn that required mowing. She owned an old hand-pushed, reel-type lawn mower, and from time to time I cut the grass for her. It was difficult for me to push the mower because the handle of that mower was the height of my forehead. I may have been ten years old at the time.

Mrs. Lockridge was a blessing to me. She gave me books and magazines to read, which helped my reading skills and increased my vocabulary and understanding. The magazines were detective-type stories and *True Confessions*. I have never forgotten one of the stories I read about a man who walked away from his wife and children, severing all contact. Some time later, his desire to see them grew strong. So he returned to where they lived. Staying out of their sight, he observed them but did not make contact. That story broke my heart.

Mrs. Lockridge also gave me books called *Big Little Books*. The stories were about western cowboys and their lives on the range. Zane Gray wrote several books about western life. He had the ability to describe a scene so vividly that I could see it. To a country boy who lived a secluded life, with no radio or television and very little connection with the outside world, these books were a godsend. Thank you, Mrs. Lockridge!

Our neighbors to the north, the Williams family, had two girls and four boys. The youngest boy was my age; he died of diphtheria at age seven. The youngest girl, Julie, was three years older than I. She and I became a team in the game of pitching horseshoes. We were pretty good at it and accepted all challenges. After we moved from the farm, she married, and I lost contact with her.

The Williams boys were hunters, and occasionally they let me tag along. These were night excursions, with light provided by kerosene lanterns or carbide lamps. It didn't take long for me to lose my sense of direction as to where my house was. My hope was that they could find it, and they did. The boys owned several dogs, and each one was trained to hunt for a particular animal, including birds, opossum, raccoon, skunk, squirrel, and rabbit. Each dog had its own particular bark, and the boys could recognize which dog was barking, saying, "Listen. That's Old Blue," or "That's Prince." From the intensity and rhythm of the bark they could also determine when the dog found the trail of its prey, when it was in pursuit, and when the prey was treed. In addition to the satisfaction they received from hearing the dogs work the way they had been trained, the boys sold the captured animals' fur for additional income. The dogs earned their room and board.

My dog, Sport, was a mixture of bull and something else. He was not a hunting dog, but he was my closest friend. Sport seldom went hunting with us because he and one of the other dogs, Buck, were prone to disagree. This distracted the other dogs, and they lost interest in hunting. When that happened, one of the boys became upset and threatened to kill Sport by shooting him with the gun he held in his hands. I was holding a .22-caliber rifle in my hands, and after some consideration—approximately two seconds—I very calmly suggested to him that if he shot my dog, I would shoot him. Thanks be to God, there was no shooting.

Good neighbors are a blessing from the lord.

MY MENTOR

Uncle Otho was my mentor. He was twelve years older than I and taught me the basics of life.

When I was growing up, many people used tobacco in their everyday lives, whether it was dipping snuff, chewing tobacco, smoking a pipe, or rolling their own cigarettes. One day when I was about thirteen years old, some older neighbor boys were visiting my uncle and standing around our water well, talking and joking. My uncle said to me, "Marvin, show these guys how you can chew tobacco." Then he cut off a chew from a plug and gave it to me. Well, I couldn't let him down in front of his friends, so I put it in my mouth and began to chew vigorously. I've never taken another chew of tobacco the rest of my life!

A neighbor of ours smoked a corncob pipe that he had trouble keeping lit. He used wooden kitchen matches to light the pipe and always seemed to be out of them. So whenever he stopped by our house, he asked for a match, and Pop would extend the box of matches toward him so he could take some. Most often he would take one-half of the box. The lesson I learned from this was to take some matches out of the box and give them to him.

When I was about thirteen years old, my uncle furthered my

education by giving me a drink of beer. It had a bitter taste, and I was not favorably impressed with it. Over the years I have drunk a few beers and learned to enjoy the flavor. But I never became a six- pack man or a Marlboro man.

When I was about twelve years old, my uncle began teaching me how to a drive a car. As I remember, he owned a 1930-model coupe of some make. He took his chances in letting me drive, but I did very well and kept the car in the road at the high rate of speed of five to ten miles per hour. My number-one problem was keeping my foot on the accelerator. The accelerator was not a flat pedal but a bare, round piece of metal about the size of a half dollar. I drove barefoot, and my foot kept sliding off, causing the car to jerk and jump. The resulting ride was very uncomfortable, like riding a bucking horse.

One time my uncle and I went motoring south on Highway 71 from Fort Smith to Greenwood. We came upon a particularly straight stretch of highway, which prompted Uncle Otho to remark about how straight it was. I replied, "If it is so straight, how come I have to keep steering the car?"

His answer, simply enough, was, "To keep it on the highway."

Gee, I wish I had thought of that.

MY PARTNER IN CRIME

My Uncle Loren was six years older than I. When he was an adolescent, I was just a pesky kid who wanted to tag along with him and his friends. His closest friend was Eldon Williams, a neighbor with access to a Ford Model T pickup truck. On occasion the truck didn't want to start and had to be pushed. I was always invited to help push—but never to go with them.

Loren and I had designated chores to do. He and Pop milked the cows, and I helped put feed into the feed trough so the cows could eat while being milked. I did whatever a boy my age could do to help, but I never did become a champion at extracting milk from a cow.

On one occasion Loren was carrying a bucket of milk in each hand; the buckets were extended at arm's length toward the ground. For some reason we were yelling at each other. Anger took over, and I threw a rock toward him. When the rock struck him in the head, his knees buckled and he crumpled to the ground, beautifully depositing the buckets of milk on the ground in an upright position without spilling a drop. Out of a desire to help him, I rushed to his side, picked up the buckets of milk and delivered them to the milk house.

One evening Loren and I had gone to the barn to do our chores. Suddenly a great idea came to us: Since no one else was around, why not smoke some tobacco? Loren had acquired a sack of Bull Durham tobacco from somewhere, along with a corncob pipe and cigarette paper for rolling your own. He gave me the choice of pipe or cigarette, but being the cool kid I was, I chose the pipe. We lit up and were puffing away when we saw Mom coming toward the barn. Quickly we extinguished our smokes and became perfect angels.

Mom stopped at the corn crib, and we joined her there. When she made a remark about our tardiness in putting out the cow feed, I opened my mouth to explain the truth to her. But suddenly everything I had eaten that day came out. There was a definite aroma of tobacco as well.

Somehow she knew we had been smoking. Moms are very perceptive.

The lesson I learned from this? Never smoke a corncob pipe unless you can properly handle the enjoyment of it.

EMPLOYMENT SEARCH

I lived with my paternal grandparents from my birth until I was fifteen years old. Mom and Pop were farmers who tilled the soil with horse-drawn tools and manual labor. They never complained. Instead they trusted the Lord God to provide for their needs and taught me to do the same.

When the United States became involved in World War II, the military needed additional training areas. The government purchased the land where my grandparents' farm was located to use as one of these training areas for the army. Mom and Pop were getting older and could no longer do the hard, manual labor that was required to farm the land. So they moved to the town of Greenwood and retired. In those days there were no retirement programs available to them. They had to live from their savings account, which was very small.

To help lighten my grandparents' financial load, I began to seek employment. But work opportunities were limited in a small town, and I began to look elsewhere. A close friend had an aunt and uncle who lived in Fort Smith. He suggested we could room and board with his aunt and uncle if we found a job nearby. But as it turned out, we were successful in securing employment at, of all places, the army base that had been activated on the land my grandparents had formerly farmed.

My job was as a busboy in the base cafeteria. In that capacity I cleaned the tables and the floor. It was not a prestigious job, but the pay was good for a fifteen-year-old. I am still amazed that I was hired, considering my age. In addition, I developed a friendship with an older gentleman who worked in the kitchen. He became a mentor of sorts as he helped me learn to handle working with other people. Whenever I needed advice about a situation and asked him about it, he willingly give me guidance. God was watching over me.

At the end of that summer, I left the job and moved to Texas to live with my dad and stepmother. The plan was for me to finish high school and help Dad on his farm. This didn't work out, however, and I returned to Greenwood, where Mom and Pop welcomed me home.

I still needed a paying job, so this time I went to Fort Smith and applied to dry cleaning establishments and bottling companies. Because I was only fifteen years old, I was turned away. But someone was willing to take a chance and hired me to work at one of the bottling companies. My job was to operate the bottling machine on the night shift.

The fall of the year approached and brought cool weather. At the bottling company word spread that there would be a reduction in the number of employees as the weather got colder. I was the youngest, so it looked like I would need a new job. I knew the good Lord was looking out for me when one of the dry cleaning establishments contacted me with a job offer.

I accepted the job at Day and Night Cleaners as a dry cleaner's helper. Part of my job was to pick up and deliver clothing from the hotels. The company provided a 1936 Ford panel van for this purpose. I did not have a driver's license, so I tried to be very cautious. One day as I was leaving a hotel and had begun accelerating to driving speed, a young boy ran from one of the buildings directly in front of me. This scared me! I jumped out of the van and began to chase after him, but he escaped. It later occurred to me that I was acting like the dog that chased the car but didn't know what he was going to do with it if he caught it.

On another occasion I was returning to the cleaners from making my deliveries. As I drove up an incline, I approached a traffic light, which I tried to get through before it turned red. A truck was in the outside lane, so I tried to accelerate to pass it. But at the same time the driver decided to pull into my lane. To avoid crashing into me the driver pulled back into his lane. The light turned red, and we both stopped. As we idled side by side, the man yelled, waved his hands, and pointed his finger at me. I didn't understand what his problem was but felt that I really needed to converse with him. So I waved my hands and pointed my finger at him. This seemed to irritate him and he began to remove himself from the truck. Realizing that this might be a good time to leave, I popped the clutch, only to have the engine die. Panic began to overwhelm me, but as the driver approached, the engine came alive. I left without saying good-bye.

Because I was a boy who grew up on a farm, I knew very little about the outside world. Working at the cleaners broadened my horizons and taught me about things to come. Approximately ninety percent of the employees at the cleaners were women because we were in the middle of World War II, and women were replacing men in the workplace. I had never been exposed to a group of working women before. I didn't know until then that they could tell dirty jokes and cuss like a man. My education into the ways of the world was expanding.

Full-time employment interfered with attending school, so I left school in the ninth grade. I liked sports, but a number of things kept me from participating. For example, if I had gotten hurt by playing a sport, I would have been unable to work and there would have been medical bills to pay. I couldn't afford either one.

Still, I played some football, basketball, and baseball before leaving school. I was good in athletics, but it was not to be. I was good in academics, in the top of my classes, but I lacked direction in the use of my talents.

MOVING ON

One day I heard that the wages for work were higher in California than in Arkansas. Since my Uncle Otho lived in Los Angeles, I wrote him a letter asking if I should come to California for a better-paying job. He advised me to wait until I was sixteen years old. That birthday came in November 1943.

I kept thinking about going to California, but I did not have any plans as to how I could accomplish this. My net income from the dry cleaners was only sixteen dollars per week. After paying for my room and board, I had seven dollars to live on. One does not build a large savings account on this kind of income.

One day I met up with a young man, Bobby Kaylor, who was two or three years older than I. At his age he was old enough for the military draft but had been rejected because of physical disabilities. I already knew him because he lived in a farming community next to the one I had grown up in. We had even ridden the same school bus. Bobby suggested we go to California, and it sounded good to me. "Let's do it," I said.

Because our country was involved in World War II, transportation was limited. Automobile production had been discontinued in favor of producing machinery for the military; gasoline, tires, and some foods were being rationed as well. To buy one of these products, a citizen had to apply for a permit. Different classes of permits were issued based on job requirements and other factors. Stamps were issued in *A*, *B*, and *C* classifications, which qualified the holder to purchase a given quantity of those products over a designated period of time.

One day Bobby saw an advertisement in the Fort Smith newspaper that read, "Traveling to Los Angeles, California. Have room for two passengers." We contacted the person, made our reservation, and found out the cost was twenty-five dollars each. I didn't have the money, but Pop Parmer loaned me fifty dollars to pay for transportation and other expenses.

Uncle Otho told me I could stay with him and his family until I found a job. He had a job lined up for me to work in a factory that produced wood doors, wood shutters, and cabinets for the housing market. Of course I started at the very top: unloading lumber from railroad cars. Well, you have to start somewhere!

Over time I worked my way into the cabinet shop, where I was classified as a cabinet-maker's apprentice. My income jumped from sixteen dollars to twenty-eight dollars per week. In a very short time I was able to repay the fifty dollars to Pop and had some money to buy clothes. My uncle took me shopping at Robert Hall Clothiers, where I purchased dress clothes the likes of which I had never seen.

In California I renewed my acquaintance with a boy whose family had moved there from Greenwood. He had a driver's license and access to his dad's car, so we went places and to the movies together. He resented me for wearing dress clothing and told me I was overdressed. But I enjoyed having some dress clothes, and I wore them.

California law required me to attend high school one day per week, so I enrolled in Metropolitan High School, which was located in the downtown area of Los Angeles. I lived in Huntington Park and don't know the distance that separated the two locations, but public transportation made it easy to move around. My employer, West Coast Screen Company, was gracious enough to allow me to take a day off to meet the school attendance requirement and to make up the lost work time by working that night.

In that era, street gangs frequented the school area. Known as *Pachucos,* these gangs were made up of Mexican-American adolescents, generally ages thirteen to twenty-two. The males wore black "zoot suits" with long coats that hung to the knees and had shoulder pads, which made the wearers look broad-shouldered. Their pants were semi-ballooned and draped down to a tight fit at the ankle. A chain extended in a loop from the waist to the knee and back to the waist. Was it an accessory? Or a weapon? Certainly switchblade knives were part of their arsenal. Thankfully I was never approached by one of them.

Besides going to Metropolitan High School, I also attended an evening class in cabinet making one evening per week at Fremont High School. Transportation involved taking the streetcar with one transfer. One evening on the way home, I arrived at the transfer point and decided to walk home from there. About one block in front of me I saw five Pachucos huddled together on my side of the street. My first thought was to cross to the other side of the street. Then I thought, *They will think I am afraid and will attack me.* As I approached them, they spread out so I had to walk directly through them, and I did. None of them moved but remained frozen in place. Was I stupid? Possibly. Was I brave? No. But I was trusting the Lord Jesus Christ to protect me, for He said He would.

A NEW WORLD

My Uncle Otho and Aunt Zella showed me a whole new world. They took me to see the ocean, where I viewed the most spectacular scene. I can still visualize it vividly. It was winter, and there no sunshine, just a dreary haze above the water. But I had never before seen a place where the water disappeared over the horizon. It was amazing!

When summer arrived, the beach frequently attracted my presence. This was the Big Band era, and my aunt and uncle also took me to see Tommy Dorsey and his orchestra and other great orchestras. My worldly education was greatly expanded when we attended a burlesque show. A beautiful woman danced onto the stage wearing a lovely dress. Without any warning the dress fell onto the stage floor, leaving her standing in only her underclothes. My first thoughts were, *How embarrassing this must be for her! Someone needs to help her get the dress back on!* But I was so embarrassed for her that I decided to keep my seat and see how she would take care of the situation. She took care of it in a way that was very entertaining.

My uncle and aunt were great to me and treated me like one of the family. I was so at ease with them that I didn't consider that I might be interrupting their family life. It was all about me and my comfort, which quickly developed into contentment. My uncle had to remind me to find my own place to live. I was blessed to find a place that was conveniently near my place of work. The room I rented was in the home of an elderly couple. They were good people, and we connected with each other.

I walked to and from work each day and became a regular breakfast customer at a local cafe. I also got to know some people who were from Arkansas who were two to four years my senior. There were two men and two women, but no romantic attraction was involved. All of us were from Arkansas and simply enjoyed being together.

On one occasion the two women and I rode a train to downtown Los Angeles to see a stage show. On our return trip we observed a man showing an interest in us. His interest did not impress us to make his acquaintance. As we disembarked the train, he did, too, and followed close behind us. Our anxiety began to increase, and we decided to confront him. When we stopped and turned to face him, he had a look of surprise on his face. He hesitated, and then he turned and walked away.

As we discussed the event, one of the girls showed us a large knife she was carrying as a weapon of defense. The other girl extracted from her clothing a larger knife, which may have been a switchblade. Until that moment, I had not known how well I was protected.

Marvin T. Parmer & Threcy Carter Parmer
Biological Mom & Dad, 1925

Dora Rush Parmer, Marvin L. Parmer & John L. Parmer
When his mom died, they became "Mom & Pop," 1942

Marvin L. Parmer & Dora Rush Parmer
In front of '40 Ford, 1947

Marvin L. Parmer
First car, '37 Ford V8, 1944

Marvin L. Parmer *(top)*, Theresa Parmer Mullins *(left)*,
Anita Boyd Parmer *(right)*, & Michael Parmer *(bottom)*

Marvin L. Parmer

Anita Boyd Parmer

The family
2010

Return Home

In December 1944 I returned home to Greenwood, Arkansas. My grandparents welcomed me with open arms and provided me with a home.

While in California I had become acquainted with some other people from Arkansas. How we met I do not remember, but one man was from Mountainburg. He was four or five years older than I and was exempt from military service. He also owned a 1936 Ford sedan with tires that were not very good. One day he said to me, "Let's go to Arkansas for Christmas." I really had not thought about making a trip home for Christmas, but the idea was very appealing.

We agreed that he and I would take turns driving so we could drive straight through. This would allow us to avoid lodging expenses and make for a faster trip. Now if we could come up with some help to pay for gasoline, we would be okay! Somehow we found a young couple who were looking for transportation to Arkansas. This worked out great because they agreed to pay twenty dollars each for their transportation. Thus we headed for Arkansas.

Due to the condition of the tires, we decided it was in our best interest not to exceed fifty-five miles per hour. After all, we were looking at a travel distance of approximately thirteen hundred miles. We knew the trip was going to take a few days, so we thought it best to relax and not be overly anxious.

One morning I was driving as the sun came up. Everyone else was sleeping, so it must have seemed appropriate for me to join them. We were driving through flat desert country, and there was nothing in our way. But when I closed my eyes, someone sneaked in a curve, and I missed it. When the car left the highway, everyone came alive, including me. There was nothing in our path to restrict our mobility, and I was able to keep the car moving. I had observed that the highway curved to the right, so I steered the car in a large radius in that direction. Would you believe that directly in front of us was the highway? The car was able to climb up on the highway, and we continued our trip.

Have I mentioned before that Someone was watching over me?

HOME IN GREENWOOD, 1945

My close friend, Warren Smith, also lived in Greenwood. He and I secured work with Wortz Biscuit Company in Fort Smith and began work together at the same time. Our job was to unload railroad cars of supplies and store them in the warehouse. These supplies were sacks of flour, sugar, and other ingredients used in the production of saltine crackers and cookies. It was hard manual labor.

Within three weeks, however, management moved both of us into the bakery. There were two large rotary ovens—one for cookies and one for saltine crackers. Warren was assigned to the cookie oven, and I was assigned to the cracker oven. His job was to place large pans of unbaked cookies into the oven and remove them when they were done. My job was to remove sheets of baked crackers from the oven and place them on the moving elevator that conveyed them to a packing area. Learning to remove a sheet of crackers—eighteen crackers wide by thirty-six crackers long—using a wooden peel (a shovel-like device) fifteen inches wide by thirty inches long, without breaking them, took awhile. But with the development of my skills and learning to control the baking process, my earnings increased from fifty cents to eighty cents per hour.

Greenwood and Fort Smith were twenty miles apart, but there was no daily public transportation. At first Warren's dad loaned us his car to drive to work, but after a short time I was able to purchase my own car. Then we alternated our transportation day by day.

Now that I had a steady income, I could afford to buy a car and purchased a 1937 Ford coupe. It was sky blue and free of any body damage—a nice-looking car. But as the old saying goes, "You can't judge a book by its cover." I got a hint of what that meant with my car. It needed tires and burned more oil than gasoline.

The year was 1945, and tires and gasoline were rationed. Thankfully motor oil was not. Depending on what his or her car was used for, a person could qualify for ration stamps. Fortunately there were two women who lived in Greenwood and rode to work with me. Because I furnished transportation for other people, I qualified for a ration stamp, which allowed me to purchase a tire in intervals of time and a designated number of gallons of gasoline within a period of time. This worked very well for me, and I bought two new tires and two used tires.

The car was equipped with mechanical brakes, with each brake attached by a cable to the brake pedal. The problem was that three of the brakes did not work, and just one brake was not very effective in stopping the car. This was brought to my attention one morning on my way to work with my two passengers on board. The highway was a two-lane concrete road. As we descended from a hill at approximately fifty-five miles per hour and rounded a curve, several horses suddenly appeared in front of us. I quickly applied the brakes, which did not slow the car to any noticeable degree. The horses were scattered far enough apart to allow me room to steer in and out and around each one of them. By the grace of God we made it through without striking a horse.

This experience motivated me to have the brakes repaired. The day I got the car out of the repair shop, I was driving north on

Midland Boulevard in Fort Smith when a car pulled out in front of me from the left. I applied the new brakes and stopped just before impact. How close were we? The end of the rear bumper on his car caught the grill guard mounted on my front bumper. He did not stop but sped away. Someone was watching over me again.

Late one night my friend Warren and I were on our way home from Fort Smith. He was asleep in the passenger seat and looked so comfortable that I was influenced to join him. When I woke up, however, there was nothing but tall weeds in front of me instead of a highway. I slammed on the brakes which caused Warren to fall out of his seat. The shock of it woke him and he asked, "Where are we?"

Giving an honest answer, I said, "I don't know."

"Where is the highway?" he asked.

Again I answered, "I don't know!"

We found the highway, and as we stood there wondering what to do, a car approached us. It was a young man we knew, and he was willing to help. We decided he could drive me to my house to get a chain. We chained the two cars together, and he was successful in extracting my car from the field. No one was injured, and the car was not damaged. Someone was watching over us!

COURTSHIP

During the months I was home in Greenwood in 1945, I met a girl named Anita (in Arkansas language "Aneeda") Boyd. She was sixteen years old, and I was seventeen. We didn't really date, but on occasion I was invited to her house along with her friends to play games. As I remember, we played a game called Spoon, which involved everyone present. It was a fun game we all enjoyed, but don't ask me how it is played. I haven't a clue!

During these months Warren and I were trying to become men. We attended western dances where we could meet girls. None of these meetings ever materialized into anything romantic for either of us. We were just kids doing what kids our age did.

The day before I left to serve in the U.S. Navy was a Sunday. Anita attended church on Sunday evening, and we were supposed to meet after church at the local café. I don't remember exactly what happened, but I didn't make it to the café in time to see her.

Some months later my ship *DE-697* was docked in Shanghai, China, alongside another destroyer escort. Aboard this ship was a schoolmate from Greenwood named C. L. Bell. We had a short time to visit, and afterward he wrote to Anita. C.L. told her he had seen me and suggested that it would be nice if she wrote to me.

I had actually written to her some months earlier, but she had not responded. I think she was a little upset with me for not meeting her at the café! But after thinking about it awhile, she decided to write. Her motive was to see if I would become interested in her. If I did, she would lead me along and then drop me with a "Dear John" letter—a letter saying, "Sorry, but I'm not interested in you after all." This was the type of letter some women wrote to their boyfriends while the men were serving their country in war.

After some months of writing to each other, I came home on a thirty-day leave from the Navy. We became better acquainted and decided we would continue to write each other. At this time she decided that dropping me was not severe enough punishment for my not showing up at the café. She resolved that marrying me and making me pay for the rest of my life would be more appropriate. So on December 18, 1948, she trapped me into saying "I do," and I have been paying ever since and enjoying it.

TOURING THE
SOUTH PACIFIC

On October 16, 1945, I boarded a Greyhound bus in Greenwood. My immediate destination was Little Rock, Arkansas, to report to the U.S. Navy district office for induction into that branch of the military. I had been told I would not need to bring anything with me because whatever I needed would be provided. So I took nothing with me, not even a toothbrush, which was not a smart move.

In Little Rock the new recruits boarded a train to San Diego, California. Our destination was the naval training base. The trip took seven days because we zigged-zagged across the country as required by our government as a war-time precaution.

I arrived on base with fifty eight cents in my pocket and the clothes on my back. True to the Navy's word, I was issued new clothing along with a toothbrush and a razor, all of which I desperately needed.

Upon completing our training, most of the company I had trained with was sent to other bases for assignment wherever they were needed. I was assigned to a ship, the *USS George* (DE-697), and boarded in San Diego Bay. Destroyer escorts (DE) are relatively small vessels and are easily tossed about by the sea—a fact I soon experienced.

Within a few days, we were dispatched to the South Pacific. Our first port of call was Pearl Harbor. The sea was restless, and we were tossed about like a floating cork. This was my first experience with seasickness. I carried a bucket with me the entire five days it took us to reach Pearl Harbor.

From Pearl Harbor we sailed to Hong Kong; to Tsingtao, China; and to Japan. We were part of the post-war patrol to make sure the South Pacific was secure.

My ship participated in the Eniwetok Atoll Operation, which was an experiment to test the effects of dropping an atomic bomb onto a floating ship. The target was a retired battleship, the *USS Nevada*. We were eighteen miles upwind from the target when the bomb was exploded. We wore special goggles so we could look at the fiery mushroom emanating from the explosion, and we could feel the heat that was generated.

Of course the target was now contaminated and had to be destroyed. The plan was to sink it into the ocean by using it for target practice. The smallest ships, equipped with the smallest guns, were first to fire on it. Then followed other ships in this order: destroyer escort, destroyer, cruiser, battleship, torpedo planes, and submarines. My ship was the flagship, and after each firing we went alongside the target to observe the damage results. It took torpedoes to sink it.

My enlistment was for three years, and I served all of it aboard the *George*. Upon receipt of my honorable discharge, I was encouraged to enlist in the Navy Reserves. The appeal sounded good, so I joined.

MAKING POINTS

In 1946 the Navy granted me a thirty-day leave. This was my first opportunity to go home since enlisting. Transportation was not readily available to me, so I went shopping for a car. I found a very nice 1940 Ford convertible at a car lot in Van Buren, Arkansas. The car was maroon with a white top and was very nice and in good running condition. I was proud to be its new owner.

Anita's dad was a road contractor who traveled to wherever the job was. Consequently, he spent a lot of time away from home. On this particular occasion he was working in Stuttgart, Arkansas. He had taken Anita's eleven-year-old brother with him so they could have some father-son time together. To drive from Greenwood to Stuttgart took about three and one-half hours. So we decided to go pick up Anita's brother and bring him home. This trip would also give us the opportunity to see parts of Arkansas we had not seen.

On the appointed day for our trip, Anita, her mother, and I loaded into my convertible and took off for Stuttgart. The car had a jump seat in the back, and somehow Anita's mother ended up in that seat. I lowered the top so we could enjoy the sun and the wind. Of course, being teenagers and having all knowledge and wisdom, we didn't consider the possibility that Anita's mother could get sunburn and windburn, which she did.

Anita's dad was lodging in an old hotel in Stuttgart. He had reserved three adjoining rooms on the third floor: one for himself and Anita's mother, one for Anita and her brother, and one for me. There was a connecting door between Anita's room and mine, so he made a big issue of checking to see that the door was securely locked. He gave his okay, and we all laughed.

Later we went to the hotel restaurant to eat dinner. Mr. Boyd suggested the fried catfish was very good. Everyone ordered catfish, but for some reason I ordered steak. This was not a smart move on my part. I wasn't making any points with my future father-in-law.

The next morning we got our things together to head back to Greenwood. Everyone gathered in Anita's room to visit while Anita and her brother packed. I decided to join them by entering her room through the adjoining door that Mr. Boyd had made sure was secure against my entry. Imagine everyone's surprise! I guess I was trying to make points with my future father-in-law by showing my skill at picking locks.

A SPECIAL OCCASION

Upon receiving my discharge from the U.S. Navy in November 1948, I returned home to Greenwood. Anita and I decided we would be married in December, but in the meantime I needed a job. This would make our marriage more acceptable to her parents.

Anita's dad had connections with Evans Coal Company, whose main offices were located in Fort Smith. He recommended me for employment, and I was hired—not as the C.E.O. with outstanding credentials, of which I had none, but as a laborer in the mine. At least I had a job!

The mine was an open pit mine located near Spiro, Oklahoma. Using county roads, which were constructed of dirt and gravel, the distance from Greenwood to the job site was approximately thirty-five miles of dust, mud, and potholes.

I was assigned to an assembly crew whose job was to assemble a new, enormous dragline, which would be used in removing dirt that covered the coal. The job was not exciting and not very laborious. It was, instead, very boring. After about four weeks I realized that I was not really needed and the job had been created for me. So, considering all things, I decided to terminate my employment. This occurred one week before our wedding, and I am sure Anita's dad wondered what kind of provider I would be for his daughter.

On December 18, 1948, a very special occasion occurred. Relatives and friends gathered at the First Baptist Church in Greenwood to witness our vows of marriage. It was an informal wedding filled with love.

Anita and her mother had secured an apartment in Fort Smith where we could begin married life together. It was a ground-floor apartment in a two-story house and was very nice and comfortable. Our wedding shower had provided us with linens and utensils to help us get started. One of several things we did not have was a bread toaster.

This omission became very important. Our first breakfast was the conventional bacon, eggs, and toast. Without a toaster, Anita attempted to toast the bread in the oven. For some reason the toast turned brown and then black. But she hung in there and finally got it right. Later that day we went for a drive, and as we were returning home, we talked about stopping at the store for a few items. Anita added, "And a loaf of bread." She then confessed that somehow the loaf of bread we had had been consumed by fire. We still laugh about this incident.

HONEYMOON

Anita was working as a bookkeeper for Evans Coal Company in Fort Smith. I needed to secure employment and was looking at possibilities. An acquaintance of mine was a cab driver in Fort Smith, and he encouraged me to try that profession. To qualify for the job, one had to be licensed by the city police department. The chief of police knew my parents, and he tried to discourage me from this occupation. However, he approved my license, and I launched into a new business.

In any new business it takes time to build a customer base. And in the meantime, it is a struggle to establish a steady income. I had not given proper attention to the fact that in order to earn a profit, I had to take in more money than I spent. Major expenses were rent and gasoline for the car. It was crucial to my well being to take in more money.

My working hours were from 3 a.m. to 3 p.m. Unfortunately this did not coincide with Anita's working hours, which were from 8 a.m. to 5 p.m. When I left for work, she was still sleeping, and when she came home from work, I was sleeping. This was not a great life for newlyweds! So I ended my taxi driving career and moved on.

Next I found employment with Acee Milk Company as a machine operator for the bottling of milk. This was a daytime job, and Anita and I could have a life together. Because I had just spent three years in the South Pacific where there was no milk to drink, I found myself trying to make up for it by including milk—a lot of it—in my daily diet. It wasn't long until the bathroom scale begin to weigh more.

During this period I applied for admission to Oklahoma A&M Technical School, located in Okmulgee, Oklahoma. In the spring of 1949 we loaded all of our belongings into the car, a 1941 Ford two-door sedan, and moved to Okmulgee. There we rented a garage apartment off campus and moved in. The ceiling was about seven feet high in the center of the living area and sloped to about five feet high at the outer wall. It didn't take us long to learn not to approach the outer wall when standing up straight.

In Okmulgee I enrolled in the school of diesel mechanics, a two-year course. My electives were business administration, math, speech, drafting, blueprint reading, electricity, and welding. I finished the course in sixteen months and was hired by a Caterpillar Tractor dealer in Oklahoma City.

During those sixteen months, our daughter, Theresa, was born. So it was a little family of three that moved to Oklahoma City. We rented an upstairs apartment located in an old two-story house. We sanded and varnished the wood floors, painted the walls, and put curtains over the windows. We had a place to call home.

A DIVERSION

One month after moving to Oklahoma City and beginning my job with the Caterpillar dealer, I received an invitation from the Department of the Navy, requesting my presence. I was given two weeks to report to the naval base at Treasure Island near San Francisco, California. Quickly we moved Anita and Theresa to Sulphur, Oklahoma, to live with Anita's parents during my absence. And two weeks later I boarded the *USS Winston* (AKA 94) and sailed for Japan. For the next ten months, we shuttled men and supplies between Japan and Korea.

After ten months in Korea, we sailed for home. Our destination was the Navy base in San Diego, California. When I learned what our time of arrival in San Diego would be, I wrote Anita with the information and suggested she obtain a room in the Grant Hotel, located on Main Street. I would meet her there.

But when I arrived at the hotel, Anita wasn't there. I called her dad, and he informed me that she could not get a reservation at the Grant Hotel and had acquired one at a different establishment. But there was a problem: He couldn't remember the name of the hotel. At least he knew it was on Main Street! I began calling hotels and finally found Anita and Theresa—at the San Diego Hotel. We have often laughed that her dad couldn't remember the name of the San Diego Hotel in San Diego.

The *Winston* was assigned to operate out of the naval base at San Diego. It was primarily involved in training exercises, which meant we sailed out to sea for a few days to train and then returned to port. This allowed me to be home most of the time. Home was a small house we were able to rent for the duration of my active duty.

When you have plans and are working to build a career and a home for your family and that life is suddenly interrupted with a life-changing event, such as a cruise in a war zone, it takes awhile to refocus. Anita and I realized all this was just a pause in our plans. We knew we had to contend with the situation and move on.

It took a few months for us to recognize the good this situation was doing in our lives. It caused us to realize how fragile life is and how quickly things can change. We both knew the Lord Jesus Christ as our Savior but had been neglectful in our relationship with him.

While living with her parents in Sulphur, Anita met a woman who befriended her and invited her to church. Anita started attending church and began working with a Sunday school class of young people. As for me, my tour of duty in Korea caused me to think about my family and the need for us to have Jesus as a part of our family.

So it was that while living in San Diego we dedicated our lives to be a Christian family and serve the Lord. As a result of that, when we returned to Oklahoma City, we became members of Exchange Avenue Baptist Church. As we participated in church activities, we became close friends with nine other couples. All of us were about the same age, and each couple was blessed with two children. We have prayed, played, cried, and celebrated together for over sixty years.

Precious memories!

JOB ADVANCEMENT

Back in Oklahoma City I worked as a diesel mechanic from 8 a.m. to 5 p.m., five days a week. My desire, however, was to become a mechanical engineer. To fulfill this dream required further schooling, so Anita enrolled me in Oklahoma City University night classes. It was known primarily as a fine arts school, but I could take basic courses there to prepare me for engineering school.

Five days a week I rushed home from work, showered, donned clean clothes, and headed out the front door as Anita handed me a sandwich to eat on the drive to school. After working all day it was very easy for me to get a little too comfortable in an air-conditioned room where sleep was waiting for me. It was especially difficult to stay awake during a lecture class. However, the professor gently awakened me by saying in a loud voice, "Isn't that correct, Mr. Parmer? Ahem!" After a few months of this routine, I had earned enough credits to enroll in engineering school at the University of Oklahoma.

During this season of working and going to school, Anita's parents moved from Sulphur to Oklahoma City. With her mother agreeing to take care of our children, Anita acquired a job as a dental assistant. The extra income she brought in allowed me to move to a job with more opportunities for future advancement.

I was hired by Gates Rubber Company, Industrial Division, as a product application engineer. Our major products were V-belt drives and rubber hose. My job was to assist customers in determining which product to use for their application. Later I was promoted to field sales for the territory of southwestern Oklahoma, with responsibility for working with consumers of Gates Products and with the distributors of these products. This experience gave me the opportunity for further advancement.

I was assigned to Molded Rubber Goods Division. The company solicited business from manufacturers of products that required parts made of rubber. Our customers were manufacturers of oil field equipment, lawn mowers, and other types of equipment. My territory was anywhere south of the Mason-Dixon Line. I traveled five days per week, leaving home early Monday morning and returning Friday evening. I was thankful to be able to be home every weekend with my family.

It became customary for Anita to pick up four hamburgers on her way to meet me the airport. She and our two children always waited for me in the baggage claim area. Then we headed home to eat our hamburgers and catch up on what had happened that week. The children and I prepared the table while Anita prepared to serve the hamburgers. On one particular evening Anita served only three hamburgers. What had happened to the fourth burger? It began to dawn on us that my end of the table had been cut off. Anita was a little too accustomed to having a family of three.

This incident awakened us to the fact that if I were going to be part of the family, I needed to be home. So I quit my traveling job and started my own industrial supply business, providing customers with V-belts, sheaves, roller chain, sprockets, bearings, rubber hose, conveyor belting, and conveyor accessories. I traveled the same area of Oklahoma that I had traveled for Gates Rubber Company, so I knew several of my customers from that time.

Since I was selling power transmission products to rock-crushing and sand-washing plants, it was only a matter of time until I got into selling crushers and washing supplies. Anita worked the order desk and became very knowledgeable about our products. One afternoon I announced I had just sold my first crusher. Anita said, "How could you? You don't know anything about crushers." Well now, you are looking at a crusher expert.

This enterprise grew into an international business, which I enjoyed until retirement.

SPECIAL SURPRISE

Upon my release from active duty in the Navy in 1952, we had returned to Oklahoma City. My previous employer, the Caterpillar dealer, had rehired me, and we settled in Oklahoma City. Anita and I purchased a lot in a developing housing addition in Oklahoma City and built a house on it. Our home was situated between two new houses that were built by the same contractor. The neighbors in these homes were our age, and we developed friendships with them.

Our neighbors to the east were very active in their church and hosted a lot of social activities. So it was not unusual to have cars parked along the street in front of our house. The busyness of our street allowed Anita to pull off a special surprise. For my thirtieth birthday, she determined to give me a surprise birthday party.

She set up the surprise by having a cousin, who was in high school, call me and ask if I would help him with some of his studies. When I agreed to help, he asked me to come to his house, giving some plausible reason as to why he couldn't bring the materials to my house. So on the evening we had agreed on, I went to his house.

After completing our study time, I left for home. When I arrived, I saw cars parked everywhere, even in my driveway. I thought, "How inconsiderate of my neighbors' guests to block me from parking in my own driveway!" Grumbling to myself, I parked down the street and walked back to my house. When I opened the door, I found a house packed with friends yelling, "Surprise! Surprise!" and singing "Happy Birthday to You."

It was indeed a big surprise to me—so much so that I forgot I was aggravated about the inconsiderate people who had kept me from parking in my own driveway.

ONE OF GOD'S MIRACLES

God has shown me His protection many times in my life. My guardian angel has been with me to protect me from several potentially disastrous situations. One of these situations particularly stands out.

Anita's parents owned a later model car than we did. One day her dad called to tell us he was going to upgrade to a newer vehicle and asked if we wanted to trade their car for ours. This would upgrade us to a newer car with low miles. We happily assented to the trade.

At that time Anita's parents still lived in Sulphur, which is approximately an hour's drive from Oklahoma City. We agreed to drive our car to Sulphur and pick up their car and made plans to make the exchange the following weekend. On Friday evening we drove to Sulphur and spent the night at Anita's parents' house. Early the next morning we headed for Greenwood, Arkansas, to visit my mom.

We had just passed through Ada, Oklahoma, and were headed east on a two-lane highway. The topography was hilly with numerous trees. As we descended a hill, my attention was captured by a construction crew that was working along the side of the highway. Since I was involved in selling construction machinery, I was curious about what kind of machinery the crew was using.

When I looked back at the highway, we had begun ascending the next hill. At the peak of that hill sat a heavy-duty oilfield winch truck, stopped in my lane. I couldn't see around the truck to check for oncoming traffic, so I applied the brakes, which did not slow the car sufficiently. The rear end of the truck still aimed directly at our car, with the space between us rapidly decreasing. I jammed down hard on the brakes. The left brakes locked, but the right side did not. We were skidding sideways toward the truck. I could see we were going to crash into the truck, hitting the passenger side of the car where my darling wife, pregnant with our first child, sat.

But suddenly the car spun farther to the left, missing the truck, coming to rest in the other lane, and facing the opposite direction. Furthermore, our car was sitting even with the truck. The truck driver looked down at me, and I looked at him. I nodded my head toward him and drove back in the direction from which we had come until I found a place suitable for turning the car around. In the meantime the truck driver moved his vehicle out of our lane of traffic, and we proceeded on our trip to Arkansas.

Safety is not found in the absence of danger
but in the presence of GOD.

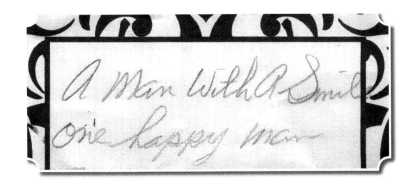

TO BE CONTINUED...

Made in the USA
San Bernardino, CA
15 July 2017